Junior MBA Seeding

A Book For The Kids

(Basics)

LalitKaushik

Junior MBA Seeding

Junior MBA Seeding

LALIT KAUSHIK

Copyright © 2024 Lalit Kaushik

All rights reserved.

ISBN: 9798338035238
Imprint: Independently published

DEDICATION

This book is dedicated to my dearest daughter Vashu Kaushik and my dearest son Kayan Kaushik. They have been my source of inspiration in writing this book, which aims to provide future perspectives of knowledge in the current time. I also dedicate this book to all the lovable kids who will choose this book as their first step in learning. May it bring them joy and knowledge.

ACKNOWLEDGMENTS

I am deeply grateful to God for providing me with the wisdom to bring the ancient Vedic tradition of learning to the new generation. I am also thankful to my beloved grandfather, Pujniye Mahrishi Vishwa Mitra Ji, and all my ancestors who have inspired and encouraged me to give selflessly to society. I am also thankful to my beloved wife, who has been a constant source of inspiration and motivation for me to write and live simply. Finally, I am thankful to all my family and friends who have supported me in one way or another.

ABOUT THE AUTHOR

Lalit Kaushik is a B.Tech. and MBA graduate, and a passionate motivational coach, motivational speaker, business coach, consultant, and best-selling book "Fun with Math" like books' author. He firmly believes that books can be a great source of motivation, enlightenment, and guidance in life. Lalit has a unique approach to helping people reach their goals and dreams, and his book is a testament to that. He deeply understands the power of motivation and how it can help people achieve their goals. He is committed to helping people reach their full potential and live a life of fulfillment.

Chapter Names

Description

Starting Fuel: Junior MBA Seeding

a) Junior MBA Seeding: Understanding Importance in 21st Century
b) The motto of a Junior MBA Seeding?
c) Is Junior MBA Seeding Required?
d) Structure of Junior MBA
   1. Planning
   2. Execution
   3. Testing
   4. Organic Sale
   5. Profit
   6. Reinvestment
   7. Marketing
   8. New Product launch
   9. Power of Feedback
   10. Few Entrepreneurs Successful stories
   11. Worldwide Few Fellowships for students
   12. How to Sterilize Pots for Safer Seed Raising
   13. Tomato

Starting Fuel: Junior MBA Seeding

Junior MBA Course: Understanding Importance in 21st Century

Guides the kids How to Recognize Opportunities– In all the life problems / requirement we may have noticed there is some pain area and solution to that So where there is a problem their solution, entrepreneurs find the answer to that. Thus, the recognition of opportunity instigates the creation of a product or service on which people become dependent. A basic rule to start this is to encourage the child to innovate ways to make good the areas of their dissatisfaction.

Solving the problem on their own: It is very important to make decisions and if the child is guided to make decisions at every step, he cannot be independent. At any sign of adversity, the child has to be ready to face it and handle it on their own. Children should be allowed to make informed decisions and be self-starters and problem solvers. For this, the child should be given opportunities where he feels independent.

Adapt to Resilience: - Resilience means adapting well in case of adversity. The child should understand that failure is part of growing and it does not matter how many times you fail if you get up and work hard again. Asking the child, the difficult areas and root cause for it and working together for it. And next learning is failure is ok until and unless you do not give up.

Help kids to start their business at an early age: The lemonade stand, renting the basketball, selling Halloween candy are examples of child business skills. It doesn't matter if it has happened numerous times or the venture is a failed business or the profit is not very good.

The activity leads to how to sell themselves and handle rejection. It also helps to overcome anxiety and concerns.

Financial knowledge: - Kids are never too young to learn about finances. And they can always learn to save money and invest in things that matter. And at the same time kids also need to understand they ca not just expect the money they have to work hard to earn it. The seeding knowledge guides the kids not to go impulsive shopping, and treat them like adults to develop the feeling of accountability for their finances.

Goal Setting is important: - Goal setting is yet another skill that is to be developed, there are lots of books that are written on goal setting. The children need to understand the concept and try to achieve it. It is easy to understand and difficult to implement the process, so if this starts at an early age the child develops the habit. Goals have to be

SMART

- S – specific
- M – measurable
- A – achievable
- R – realistic
- T – timely or time-based

This can be started by completing the to-do list which may comprise doing math homework, eating lunch, reading a book, etc.

Technology Skills: - In this 21st century world of technology the children are exposed to tech-savvy things. Computers are an essential part of our life and children must know how to operate those things. Some games and coding involve in-depth computation and reasoning that is needed in almost every profession. Exposure to those helps to develop logic and creativity.

The Junior MBA seeding is initial food for future entrepreneurs by Lalit Kaushik having years of experience and this beginning includes very simple home base experiential learning even role-plays are an important part of it through which children demonstrate the skills learned. The chapters are unique and special focus for motivation on each step so that the child feels independent and develops confidence.

This book is specifically designed keeping in view the age group and ways that can make learning fun.

Once you complete this book, you will be amazed by the overall performance of your child.

The motto of a Junior MBA seeding?

- Transferable skills
- Networking opportunities
- Decision-making skills
- Degree specializations

Transferable Skills
It provides new skills and knowledge to our Junior MBA Course holders to achieve more knowledge about the current

industry and Entrepreneurship. The hard and soft skills that they acquire during the course will help in other roles. They are a larger number of MBAs who are working in tech, health care, consumer goods, government offices, and many other industries.

The skill that they acquire during the course will give them the strength to learn leadership, analysis, creative thinking, cultural awareness, and communication, it will also help you find your way toward your goal.

Networking Opportunities

Since our kids are already aware of social media and technology and its function. At a business seeding, they will interact closely with talented individuals from all over the world, which will help them to experience, and expose to different business practice, culture, and their points of view. Our Junior MBA students will be able to solve any hypothetical or uncommon challenge with the skills that they acquire in this Junior MBA seeding. It will help them to learn new skills, implement programming and management skills. The connections you make also helps you to learn the most valuable aspects of Junior MBA, make sure you utilize the time in and out completely to gain more knowledge through networking.

Decision-Making Skills

Junior MBA improves the skill of decision-making by-themself at a certain point it may be professional or personal with which they would learn to take a risk also helps them to be self-dependent It also helps them to examine the situation in life before making any decisions in life which will help them to learn about money, time, and resource management factors through Junior MBA seeding.

Junior MBA Seeding

Degree specializations

It is very important to make our Junior MBA students go through this book. It is a very precious designed to deliver a Junior MBA style curriculum to school students.

The main motto is to deliver the Junior MBA modules to children aged 6-15 years with four learning goals. To encourage students to think critically to provide basic management literacy skills to students to encourage collaboration among students to improve the presentation skills of students. The junior MBA seeding is considered essential for students as it provides them not only with financial literacy skills and helps them with entrepreneurship which will help them in the long run.

Note: Reference
1 :https://www.henryharvin.com/blog/give-your-children-the-financial-edge-with-the-junior-mba/

Is Junior MBA Seeding Required?

Yes, it is very much required for our kids. Since I have come across many people who would have trained to be Doctors, Accountant, IPS Officers, Engineer, or Lawyer. Later they would have sifted to move into business. The reason is real calling was actually for entrepreneurship.

If you ask the middle age people who would have not been exposed to early in their life to become entrepreneurship until they took an MBA after their graduation. They would have known business by playing the business game or Monopoly in their lifetime.

Later they have realized that 'selling' or 'management' was their calling.

Today's children have an advantage to sneak-peak into different types of education like Junior MBA seeding. Junior MBA seeding program helps them to improve their management of business skills while they are in the school itself. This will help our students to make a well-informed and timely decision about their career without wasting time.

Structure of Junior MBA Seeding

The Junior MBA seeding program is a self-esteemed program that makes our kids face real-life case studies and help them to understand the working of corporate houses in a simple language. For example, successful business models like OYO, Vedanta, and Ola.

This will also help our Junior MBA to expose to how business can have a positive impact on society by way of step-by-step learning.

The Junior MBA seeding helps our kids in their creativity as well as their entrepreneurship skills and help them evolve their business sense. Junior MBA seeding program helps children develop confidence and a sense of collaboration. Which will help them to prepare for the personal, academic, and professional journey ahead?

The Junior MBA is offered from level one and goes through areas like finance, management, marketing, and other aspects of a business.

The main goal of the Junior MBA seeding book is to train the students at an early age so that they can develop the required skills at an early stage.

- Their mind will develop to think critically
- It also provides students with basic skills beyond their age and ability
- It also enhances their presentation skills
    - Learn to work as a team with team spirit

Junior MBA Seeding

Junior MBA seeding book is designed in such a way that they are focusing on the age group and their level of understanding of the school students.

Chapter 1. Planning

Planning is about what steps you need to take to reach the goal, what changes and hurdles to anticipate, and how to utilize human resources and opportunities to reach the expected outcome.

In this chapter we understand as a parent many questions before jump into conclusions or action.

- What we understand about planning?

- What is the need of planning?

- How it works?

- What is the relation between planning and seeding of business skill in initial stage in kids?

What we understand about planning?

If you are not a working woman or a small vendor or a farmer, you need not to be worried about to understand planning. Actually, most of the persons are familiar and expert in this without aware of technical understanding. In eye of our mothers and sisters planning is the subconscious part activity. You do not believe? Soon you will start believing. In our families we see mother wake up early in the morning and start all activities of the day for her children, husband and family without noticing them. For school going children she ready brunch and school tiffin and wake up all school going kids as per planning of their routine time require to accomplished the task. Similarly serve brunch to all whether school going or office going. After one activity she start to do another activity of the day either office going preparation or other. She smartly handles all activity of the day with simile. until all going on a bed, she continuously serves each one. Can you observe how she maintain such a tedious task without any pain or tension?

It is very simple to understand in eye of management that is planning. As she understands what activity start first and what parallel or what next and last. Moreover, she understands what outcome will come out from the action. Even some times she fails to attempt to do anything on time or properly due to any reasons whether due to late night party or some unusual guest at home, she covers up without any highlighting with smartness. In simple terms we call Mothers planning and her management.

Similarly, as farmer, he /she plant when to seed or when watering and process other activity.

Benefits of Planning

It Helps to Set the Right Goals

It Sets Objectives and Standards for Controlling

It Reduces Uncertainty

It Eliminates Overlapping of Wasteful Activities

It Ensures Efficient use of Resources

It Promotes Innovation

It Improves Decision Making

It Boosts Motivation and Team Spirit

It Helps to Earn Credibility and Trust of Stakeholders

It Gives a Competitive Edge and Allows Strategic Positioning

Here we have to plan how to seed a business acumen inside child.

We have to plan first what item we can sale initially. As per writer you can start with kitchen vegetables like tomato, chilly, lemon, paper mint, coriander etc. or in fruits we can start with orange, guava etc. The selection purely based on interest and daily requirement. Once we freeze the procedure of next planning is where we have to arrange seed for seeding

Why we choose above mentioned item?

As you are aware during seeding, we understand we will become first consumer in alternate mechanism. For example, in kitchen we consume around 2-3 tomatoes daily in habitual essential practice in India or around the India. Similarly, lemon, Potato, which is modified stem etc. In conclusion we have to choose seeds of those whose product we are consuming daily in a kitchen whether herbs or shrubs.

Where will we get seeds of selected item?
It is good question to be understand. For this we suggest to prepare

seeds at home or purchase online. Various sites are available who sale online seeds packet. Most important point is quality of seed. How will you select good quality seeds? We suggest to prepare high quality seeds at home from our daily items. (Details of few items attached in last)

How can we prepare seeds at home?

For this remove without damage seeds from fruit and vegetables consume in kitchen in following manner.

First: Remove and clean the seeds
Second: Dry and store for long term use.

Prepare Soil

Soil is the important factor for seeding. For considering good quality outcome, plan for soil quality. What question we ask for during soil preparation?

- What type of soil we require?
- What other ingredient will be the part of soil?
- How much quantity we require?
- What other item we require for holding soil?

In chapters we will understand in depth all question answers.

Seeding the seed

This is very crucial for real outcome in the form of product. During seeding we have to plan and prepare for following questions answer in detail.

- When we have to seeding the seed?
- How we seeding the seed?
- What safety we have to plan for better seeding, before and after?
- What other activity we have to start immediately, if any after seeding?

Wait and learn patience

Really is it essential to learn?

Nurture day to day requirement of plant

Time to start to plan about testing of your product

Plan to sale your product

Junior MBA Seeding

Search open second level market

Plan to reinvest

Plan to energies production

Enjoy feedback on timely basis.

Reference:

a) https://peoplemanagingpeople.com/tools/hr-software/

Chapter 2: Execution

Purchase of raw material

Once planning is over. The next move starts to buy all raw materials like,

a) Suitable size pots if vacant land is not available in home
b) Soil
c) Green or organic Manure
d) Seed
e) Support if your plant (under category of climber Either Herbs or shrubs) require
f) Water sprayer

As our planning gives us good confidence of all step. Now the time to work with your child in buying of above-mentioned items. Now first give money as per planned to him with some extra one and go to the market where we will purchase all items as per plan. In this we must remember all items correspondence ought to be done by child with seller. However, as a parent you give in depth learning before going to the market. Following question must be attended with kids.

Q 1: What is pots?

Q2: Material of pots?

Q3: Where possible we can buy these pots either online or offline?

Q4: How can we consider quality perspective in mind during purchasing?

Q5: How can cost be a part of buying of pots including transportation?

Q6: Type of Soil?

Q7: How much soil we require for pots?

Q8: What type of green/organic manure we require for seed?

Q9: Can we prepare at home or suitable buy from the market?

Q10: What is the cost at home and in market?

Q11: Item which we have planned to seed as per kitchen daily requirement or planning?

Q12: Where we can get best seed either from home or marked considering quality of seeds?

Q13: Cost of seed in both conditions either you developed at home or buying from the market.

Q14: Size of water sprayer?

Q15: Material of water sprayer?

Q16: Where we can get our selected one water sprayer?

Q17: If support is required then following queries must be a part of understanding.

- Size of support
- Material of support etc
- Cost
- Market where we can get

You will be surprised once you will give the insight of information to your kids. Do not give information in hurry every chapter has a unique learning to your kids. Most important thing is your child will be charged in every step and give a positive signal of interest in regular study too.

Give a child proper time to understand answer of all queries as per planning and take him or her test as you take during preparation of conventional exam. For your easiness we have given some organic test series at the end of each chapter. But it is not necessary to ask only these one you decide better as per your planning. The main purpose of test is just to understand how much your kid learn or understand these points. Make sure do not discuss about technical names in initially. Always give last the name of each step once it is successfully over so that your kid under stands the power of every step.

During buying from the market give free hand to your kids for bargaining and ask minimum for three places of seller, so that he/she can analysis every point of learning. Do not interrupt if he/she chose costliest one during purchase as it may be a logical one when you will ask once purchasing is over and ask why you chose this one? If you are not satisfying give them proper justification once again and tell to highlight this error in record.

If you want to buy any seed online, you can take help of google online site or take from Indian site like

- https://seed2plant.in

Process of raw material

In this we start seeding the seed in pot or available land at home for gardening. We prefer you seed in pots as we can relocate as per the photon's requirement from the lord sun. As you are aware in the presence of chlorophyl and sun light plants prepare a food.

The process of photosynthesis is commonly written as:

$$6CO_2 + 6H_2O \rightarrow C_6H_{12}O_6 + 6O_2$$

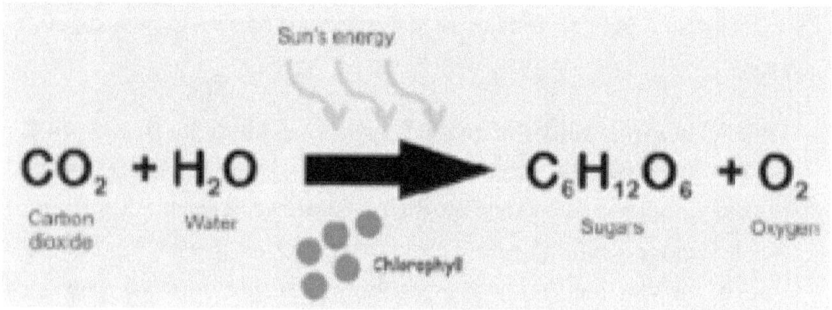

Initially put pot in normal area where sun rays are only fall in morning and evening time so that seed get suitable environment as per their category. As we are taking kitchen product suitably, we have considered tomato seeds.

Fix the drainage

Make sure your container has a hole at the bottom to allow excess water to drain out. This will prevent water from stagnating around your plant's roots and causing them to rot. The drainage hole should be as obstruction-free as possible, to allow excess water to drain out when the pot is overwatered. You can use a handful of pebbles, or place broken pot or tile pieces around the drain hole to make sure soil doesn't clog.

Prepare Soil with fertilizer

Here's the slightly tricky part. Your soil or potting medium has to have a judicious balance of organic matter, minerals, air and water. Compost generated from your home waste can easily provide the organic matter that your soil needs, while sand and cocopeat – sourced responsibly, are great soil aerators. A combination that works reasonably well for most plant types is red earth, cocopeat (or sand) and compost in the ratio 2:1:1. You can up the sand quotient for cacti and other succulents. If you'd rather not go to the trouble to source these media individually, you can select from Karnival's collection of fertilizers and ready-mixed potting media.

Put soil in pot with fertilizer

Aerate your planting medium by raking it, or even tossing it in the air until it becomes light and crumbly. Fill your container up to the brim, leaving about 3cm from the top for watering

Junior MBA Seeding

Put Seed in a pot

Plant your sapling firmly in the center of the pot. Press the potting medium firmly around the base of the plant and water the pot lightly until you see the water draining out at the bottom.

Watering

Water your plant only when the top surface of the pot looks dry. Give the drain hole a poke with a pencil or stick to check for stagnating water. Don't overwater your plant, though, especially if it's a succulent or a cactus. You only need to water succulents a couple of times a month at the most.

Fertilizer

Give your pot a pinch or two of home compost or vermicompost every three months or so. These super lightweight composters are perfect for home gardening and composting. Get some today!

Waiting Period

Waiting period is those time when you have to wait for fruit in the form of final product. Here tomato is our final product. It will take own time, there is no standard time but you have to learn to be patient and utilize this time to move one step further that is marketing of the product. Here we can utilize planning and hiring someone for marketing. But for kids' perspective we have no other option to wait as kids are not aware about these terminologies and cannot bear pressure of the same.

Meanwhile prepare some product poster and mention innovative lines for future marketing. It will give kids a great knowledge of the product. Which ultimately give mastery over other. Even they can think creatively for promotion.

Following suggestive ways of creative marketing

Punch line: Few suggestive punches line

- Organic Tomato for long life
- High quality tomatoes for your health
- Have you eaten natural organic tomatoes

Further this is the time to learn more and more about your final product aspects. If you think any innovative ideas, then write down and discuss with other ones of your team

More than half the tomato production happens in China.

Tomato is an essential edible fruit also used as a vegetable in many cuisines around the world. Tomatoes are grown in temperate climates and greenhouses. More than half the tomato production happens in China. In many parts of the world, the tomatoes produced are consumed locally due to limitation in storage, limited value and shelf life.

Tomatoes are used in making ketchup, hot sauce, tomato sauce as well as tomato paste. The universal production and use of tomatoes has made tomatoes a national vegetable in many countries. In fact, La Tomatina is a tomato festival celebrated in Bunol, Spain at the end of August every year.

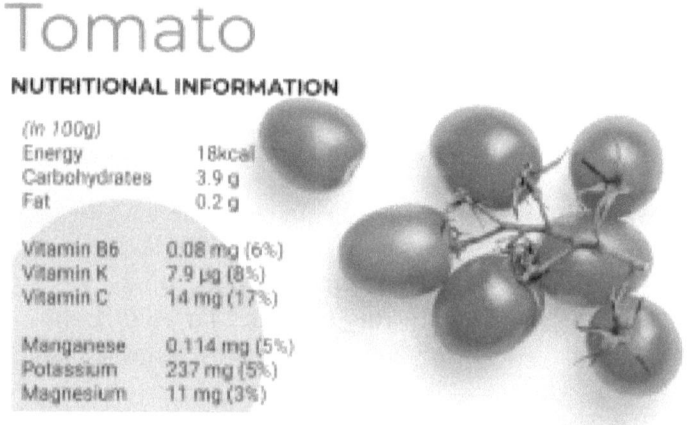

Various types of tomatoes are grown including plum, cherry and grape types of tomatoes. San Marzano is a plum variety of tomato known for its use in Pizza. Popular commercial tomato cultivars include Adoration, Alicante, Big Beef, Brandywine, Campari, Celebrity, Great White, Matt's Wild Cherry, Plum tomato, Roma, San Marzano, Santorini, Tomaccio, Tomkin and Super Sweet 100.

Testing

It is very crucial as it will decide the fate of the product and their company. In this we do following action for the testing of the product.

a) Give final product for testing after self-test
b) Give it to maximum testers
c) Continue test as many as can
d) Take feedback on standard questionnaire. For this prepare standard questionnaire.
e) Choose only for those who understand your product and expert to be testing
f) File all feedbacks in a file for review. Once you satisfy in testing go ahead for marketing
g) During testing if possible take lab test report for scientific authenticity with following test

    i. Minerals and vitamins
    ii. Fats
    iii. Carbohydrates
    iv. Any other nutrition
    v. Life of product in open
    vi. Life of product in favourable condition
    vii. Take toxicology report of product

In your mind many questions will arise, it is obvious. Do not stop these are natural when we are taking interest in any topic, in curiosity we will ask many questions. Few questions here we are attempting.

Q1: Why we need testing before launching a product?

Product testing is the process of gathering feedback directly from customers or potential customers about a product. The feedback can be through informal conversation, formal surveys, or even indirectly through data about clicks on an online advertisement or traffic to a website.

Product testing can happen both before and after the official launch, all the way from the initial idea stage to the prototype to the finished product. In the beginning, product testing helps businesses to determine the viability of the product.

Moving closer to the launch-ready version, product testing identifies ways to further improve on what's already been built.

Q2: Why it is important?

Throughout your business planning and especially before you launch, it's crucial to get an outside perspective on your product. What's more, you need to get to know the market. Otherwise, your online business may flop, flushing away all your invested time and money.

Although it may seem like a lot of initial effort, planning and seeking out market insights ahead of time will save you a lot of time and money in the long run.

Still on the fence about testing? Take the example of Zappos. Now an online shoe business bringing in more than a billion dollars each year, Zappo's success was not guaranteed from the beginning. When Nick Swinmurn started the company in 1999, the idea that people could buy shoes online was doubt worthy.

So, Swinmurn decided to test his product idea. Instead of tying up a lot of money in inventory, Swinmurn went to local malls, took pictures of the shoes there, and uploaded the pictures to the Zappos website.

When someone bought a pair of shoes through his website, he returned to the stores to buy them at retail price. This strategy helped Swinmurn prove that people would buy shoes online.

In addition to testing his concept, Swinmurn also studied the market, industry, and competition. He realized that people were already buying shoes from catalogues at rates of $2 billion per year, 5% of all shoe sales. By entering the growing online marketplace, Zappos could attract a large portion of those sales.

The lesson from Zappos is that learning about the market and testing your idea is both essential to get your business off the ground in an efficient and budget-conscious way. Keep reading for tips on how to do market research and ideas to test your own product.

Q3: How to test a product before launch?
Ans:

- **Prototype-Based Product Testing**
- **Market Testing**

Prototype-Based Product Testing

Now that you're pretty sure you have a killer idea and you've done your homework on the market, you're ready for product testing. By collecting feedback from potential customers, product testing enables you to hone your idea, create different versions of your product, and decide which version is best.

Junior MBA Seeding

In contrast to the idea stage, by this time you have a prototype of your product. If your product is digital, then you have a beta version of your app or website.

Next, invite people to try out your product. Be selective when choosing who you want to try the prototype or participate in your beta test. Ideally, this group should be from your target audience. If they like your product, they can recommend it to others in the future.

Then, conduct post-use surveys. Be sure to ask your test group their opinions on how the product works, what they think of the design, and their other feelings about the product

Market Testing

The last stage prior to full launch is market testing. Although related to product testing, market testing–also known as soft launch–is not the same. Product testing involves asking people about your product.

Market testing is when you launch your product in a limited area for a set period of time. With market testing, you can learn how the product actually performed in sales.

Your market test should involve the core aspect of your product. A more complete version or additional features can come later.

Although you are not getting direct feedback about specific aspects of your product to improve, you may notice that your product is performing better or worse than you expected. This information will help you to improve both your product and your marketing strategy.

Here we have consider product Tomato . Thus it is the time of testing. In this we will start from our self-testing . For this tell your kids first delivery or first day will be free of cost so that you can tell him/her true testing feedback of received product. Here 'Tomato is our testing product. On first day testing give your true views with your kid and tell each details in in depth detail. Once you tell him or her to take one more testing with in family or near and dear ones. Thus in similar fashion your kid will get true feedback under testing. If possible take lab test report too for confidence and risk minimization . However for agriculture products it must be a part of practice. As some times Microbes in agricultural production are often considered to be challenging and 'scary'. Whole microbial pathogens are known for the their problems – from Listeria on fruit, blight and rot in fields, Salmonella and E. coli outbreaks, to tainted dairy products. Other microbes are required for quality products but are challenging to quantify.

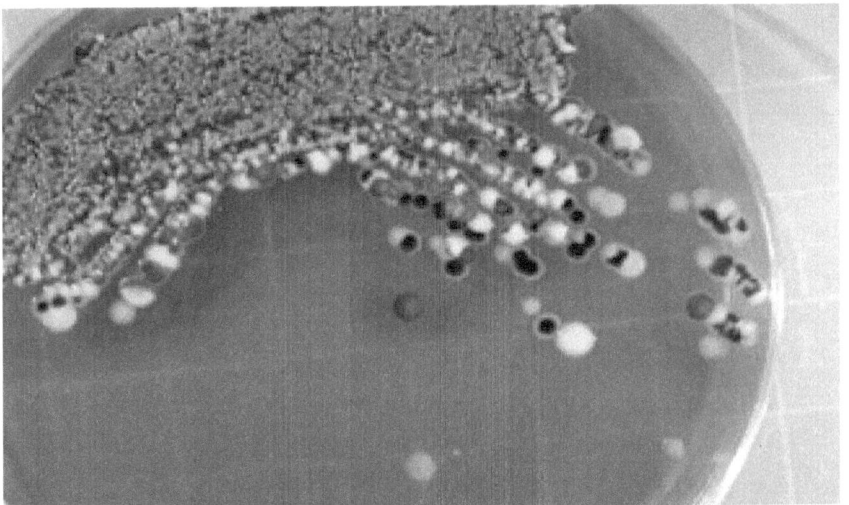

Salmonella bacteria and other bacterial pathogen outbreaks affect the livelihood of suppliers and consumers with potential long-impact on their product brand.

Junior MBA Seeding

These challenges are not limited to fields and processing plants. The tremendous amount of organic and inorganic materials used in agricultural production has to go somewhere after use. And that 'somewhere' typically involves microbes.

Microbes are at the base of a complex series of bio-chemical interactions that include fertilization, biocidal applications, composting, waste disposal as well as the use of soil amendments to boost production and enrich soils.

At each step of the process, having an understanding of the role microbes perform in agricultural production is important.

As with many other markets, knowing how to reduce possible challenges as well as how to harness microorganisms for potentially beneficial uses is not easy.

Conclusion: Once we have enough positive feedback through feedback and lab report, we can move on for holistic or organic sale. If not satisfy with product result, try investigate where is the flaw and start once again by correction in flaw until you will satisfy with your product. I can assure it will open the gate of thinking level of your kid as this stage they are not aware what exactly testing do for product. But once you will guide your kids that is similar to your examination where you work hard and attempt your exam paper but due to some unfortunate paper will not be qualify with flying colors. Then you work hard until you clear with flying color. It is really interesting learning and give your kid a better understanding.

Chapter 4: Organic Sale

Organic sales are revenues generated from within a company. Organic sales encompass those streams of revenues that are a direct result of the firm's existing operations as opposed to revenues that have been acquired through the purchase of another company or business unit in the past year. The sale or disposal of business lines are also netted out of a total sales figure to derive organic sales. Measuring organic sales is important because it can show the amount of growth that's the direct result of a company's business plan or sales strategy.

Understanding Organic Sales

Organic sales are the product of the internal processes of a company and are generated solely within the firm. Organic sales provides management and investors with the level of revenue that was generated from the sale of a company's products and services. If a company generates increases in organic sales, it's typically referred to as organic growth. Revenue growth from organic sales is usually measured on a year-to-year basis, but many companies also monitor organic growth from quarter-to-quarter.

Organic Sales Growth Strategies

Companies might achieve organic growth of their sales through internal strategies such as:

- New product and service offerings
- A marketing campaign for a particular offer to customers and prospects
- Optimization of internal processes, which might involve boosting efficiency by making changes to the internal structure of a company
- A new sales strategy with commissions or bonuses to employees who hit sales targets

- Reallocating resources, such as sales and marketing staff, to products and services that are in higher demand

Q: What are the Benefits of Organic Sales?

It's important for investors to be able to separate organic sales from sales that came from an external source. Organic sales figures will show how much revenue the company is generating from its core operations from period to period.

Real World Example of Organic Sales

PepsiCo Inc. (PEP) is a global leader in the beverage and snack business and active in trading assets through acquisitions primarily. Pepsi had recently closed its acquisition of Rockstar Energy Beverages in 2019. However, the company's Q1-2020 earnings report shows that Pepsi reported *organic revenue growth* of 7.9% compared to Q1 of 2019.1

Here we want to understand organic sale of our 'Tomato' means a lot to our kid. In this we insist to sale daily tomato organically to you as a first customer. It means you have pay as per market or fixed price during planning. Kindly guide not to spend this money until you guide to him/her a next step. Similarly give idea for organic sale with other family members in your family for different kitchen. But make sure organic sale covers only up to supply limitation . If you have two family daily supply quantity of tomato. Then you have to sale in organic up to two only and if you have quantity for five you have to sale organically up to five. Sale organically until your kid understand the real enjoyment of sale . In this you will be amazed the potential of sale will give more confidence than earlier. Once you feel he/she feel enough confidence , move to next level.

Conclusion: In organic sale your kid will learn a lot especially tactic of organic sale and will earn confidence and one best skill of sale. You will be surprised that you are well aware of this concept in many ways like you have attended baby shower, ritual program, opening of new store in your family or relation etc. where you contribute in any manner either by purchasing or by gifting.

Reference:

https://www.investopedia.com/terms/s/sale.asp

Junior MBA Seeding

Chapter 5: Profit

Profit is the money a business pulls in after accounting for all expenses. Whether it's a lemonade stand or a publicly-traded multinational company, the primary goal of any business is to earn money, therefore a business performance is based on profitability, in its various forms.

The word "profit" comes from the Latin noun *profectus*, meaning "progress," and the verb *proficere*, meaning "to advance."

Gross, Operating, and Net Profit
The first level of profitability is gross profit, which is sales minus the cost of goods sold. Sales are the first line item on the income statement, and the cost of goods sold (COGS) is generally listed just below it:

Gross Profit = Revenues - COGS

For example, if Company A has $100,000 in sales and a COGS of $60,000, it means the gross profit is $40,000, or $100,000 minus $60,000. Divide gross profit by sales for the gross profit margin, which is 40%, or $40,000 divided by $100,000.

Operating profit removes operating expenses like overhead and other indirect costs as well as accounting costs like depreciation and amortization. It is sometimes referred to as earnings before interest and taxes, or EBIT.

Operating Profit = Revenue - Cost of Goods Sold (COGS) - Operating Expenses - Depreciation & Amortization

Net profit furthermore removes the costs of interest and taxes paid by the business. Because it falls at the bottom of the income statement, it is sometimes referred to as the firm's "bottom line."

Net Profit = EBIT - Interest Expense - Taxes

The bottom line tells a company how profitable it was during a period and how much it has available for dividends and retained earnings. What's retained can be used to pay off debts, fund projects, or reinvest in the company.

Here we can understand profit means what we are earning from organic sale when we pre-assume that no initial expenditure as this is for learning. However better if cut 20 to 30 % amount for all initial expenditure. That means our profit is 70 to 80 % we considering just for kids learning about concept of profit. For more detail we take one example

Let us suppose we have considered 100 gm tomato cost $10 and it is daily consumption of one family. Our production is limited to 3 family in initial stage.

That means by organic sale your kid will earn $10 x 3 family= $30

Consider 30% All expenditure(Raw material cost+ Man & Machinery cost + water cost + marketing cost + transportation cost + other)= $9

As we know Profit= Total Earning- Total expenditure

Thus on putting the value=$30-$9-$21

Wow your kid start earning profit $21 in a day. Which is equal to 70% profit ---(A).

In second step once your kid understand **Profit meaning**. First you appreciate by little token of appreciation by small party as a parents. Now the time has come when you have to move on for next concept that will be more important in business. That is reinvestment.

Conclusion: Here we have understand basic profitability concept without technical in-depth of cost recovery through break even. Which will be attained in next level. You will be surprised your kid now grasping skill of business without official teaching in big colleges. For testing we have given practice exercise of basic level problems just for concept. Remember your kid will not only learning business acumen(MBA) through this learning but also earning lot of confidence which ultimately give overall development either in sport or academic.

Chapter 6: Reinvestment

Reinvestment is a great way to significantly increase the value of a stock, of the same investment. In business, it is very critical learning many businesses never understand the value of reinvesting due to which they come into the trap of financial crisis or some time bank loan trap.

In general term invest what we are earning into our business again and again until our business running on self-reliance mode financially. It has a magical impact; your kid soon releases the power of it. However, during initial stage, kid will not be a happy as you will giving learning about to reinvest on running business instead to enjoy the profit. But make sure your expenditure covers all expenditure along with your motivational expenditure. For me my motivation is other happiness some time some outing food with my near and dear ones. Thus, we can say everyone has different motivational forces, which must be considered since beginning. Without this expenditure we cannot pre assume growth of business. But remember that must be a minimum in initial stage. For your best learning you can tell story of Google where they did party every evening just to motivate self and there partners since beginning. Even they continue such tradition all in offices. Similarly, many top companies around the world following tradition of motivation where any one employee can do what he/she want to do for motivation. Ultimately their companies growing in compounding way.

Here in earlier chapter, we understood what was profit. Now what is the use to sell the tomato. In example (A) your kid earning in a day in initial level $21. That means in a month of 30 days, your kid will earn

=$21*30

=$630

Can you imagine that huge sum of money on reinvesting will grow your production capacity in compounding way. Through this you will be able to cater as many as can. Every time your business will grow when demand will increase. Here you will not be in pain due to financial constraint. However, banks always ready to cater your business needs. But here we insist to guide your kid about to choose last opportunity to take loan in any condition. Reinvestment is also a self-banking practice through own feet. It is a million-dollar practice in business. In India we were practicing even in the Harappa civilization this type of reinvestment of profit. Even in today's pandemic time only those business is surviving those follow reinvestment procedure. However, you and your kid may be asked some queries. Do not be worried about these queries but appreciate to yourself and your kid on queries. For resolving queries read books as many as can. Queries are the first and positive step of focused learning. However, we will address here many queries as can

Q1: Is it essential to follow reinvestment ethics in business?

No there is no essential ethics to follow reinvestment in business.

Q2: If business not in profit can we follow reinvestment ethics?

If you are running any business. The first condition is to earn the profit whether you are showing in account book or not. If not earning profit, first you have to understand the meaning of profit and procedure of earning.

Q3: If we are not earning profit in initial time during early days of business, what ought to be our strategy to come on

profit level?

For this you have to do some exercise about to get facts of not earning profit. If all are in line then investment either self or through financers is only the procedure.

Q4: Will as a businessman, have we to continue reinvestment? If yes for how many times?

Already we have told you for initial it is boon for the business. Once your system generates enough profitability after reinvestment then only you can downsize it or down the pace. But we insist try to continue it. However, you can reduce and increase considering other expenditures in business.

Q5: What will be the benefits to the end consumers from the reinvestment?

You will be surprised it give you more leverage in business as your profit will be compounding increases. As you understand business means in Snatani sanskriti is holistic or pure means only. If your business does not consider this holistic snatani view that means you are not doing business. Thus, you will reduce cost of the product so that your customer will get more value for money in holistic manner.

Q6: As a kid seeding of reinvestment skill will give any new look in general life?

Yes, it will give your kid save lot and invest lot. In directly it will learn how to invest in plan manner for long term gain.

Chapter 7: Marketing

After organic sale and we understand all pros and cons of the sale. Now the time has come when you stop spoon feeding and fly with own feather. For this you have to sale your product to unknown. Now how your customer will know about your product and their properties in terms of quality. We insist first you recall, how you buy new product in the market. In this we found different medium through which you come across of that product. Few are mentioned below

    A) Through TV advertisement

    B) Through poster

    C) Through Facebook / WhatsApp /twitter/Instagram

    D) Mouth publicity

    E) Radio

    F) Programme like match

    G) Etc.

These tactics of showcase your product come under ambit of marketing.

Marketing is the activity, set of institutions, and processes for creating, communicating, delivering, and exchanging offerings that have value for customers, clients, partners, and society at large.

Or

In other word, it is the art of showcase your product to the customer such a way so that on requirement they can buy it.

Marketing Strategy

What is marketing strategy?

A marketing strategy is a long-term plan for achieving a company's goals by understanding the needs of customers and creating a distinct and sustainable competitive advantage. It encompasses everything from determining who your customers are to deciding what channels you use to reach those customers.

With a marketing strategy, you can define how your company positions itself in the marketplace, the types of products you produce, the strategic partners you make, and the type of advertising and promotion you undertake.

Having a marketing plan is essential to the success of any business. Read on to learn how to create a successful marketing strategy for your company.

Key takeaways

- Marketing is more than just advertising and promotion – it's all about connecting with the customer.
- A marketing strategy sets the direction for all your product and marketing-related activities.
- Having a marketing strategy helps keep all your activities on track.
- Developing a marketing strategy involves setting goals, researching the market, developing product plans, defining your marketing initiatives, and following the "7 P's."

What is included in a marketing strategy?

In essence, a marketing strategy determines the general direction – but not the specific details – for a variety of marketing-related activities. Ideally, your marketing strategy should help you define the following for your company:

- Target audience
- Value proposition
- Product mix
- Brand messaging
- Promotional initiatives
- Content marketing

How to create a successful marketing strategy

There are several steps you need to take to create a robust marketing strategy for your business.

- **Set definable business goals**

    Your company's vision and objectives are the driving factors behind your marketing strategy. These overall objectives help determine your marketing goals, which your marketing strategy is in service of.

    Your marketing goals build on your company's goals. You might set a goal to achieve a specific market share, dominate a particular channel or reach a certain percentage of a certain type of consumer. Your goals should be reachable and measurable.

- **Identify and research the target market**

  The goals you set help you define the target market to pursue. This requires you to get familiar with the customers in this market, which requires some degree of market research and analysis. You need to determine the following about the target market and its customers:

    - Market size and growth potential
    - Market trends
    - Competitors
    - Geographic and demographic characteristics
    - Customer behaviour

- **Focus on the 7 P's**

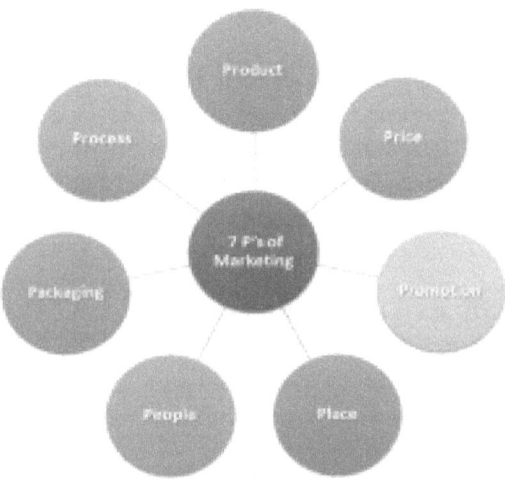

As you develop your marketing strategy, you should focus on the traditional 7 P's of marketing:

- **Product** – how you satisfy customer needs
- **Price** – how much customers are willing to pay for your product
- **Promotion** – which channels you use to tell customers about your product
- **Place** – where you sell your product
- **People** – individuals who help sell your product to customers
- **Packaging** – how you present your product to the customer
- **Process** – how you deliver your product to customers

- **Develop product plans**

    Once you understand your target customers, you can determine what products best serve those customers' needs. When you know what a customer wants, you can build the right product for that customer.

    Developing the product falls outside the parameters of the marketing department, of course, as does producing the product. But marketing should have a prominent and vocal role in determining the product's features, pricing and packaging, as determined by customer needs and metrics.

- **Identify the key benefits**

    Savvy marketers know that new customers don't make decisions based on a new product's features but rather on how that product benefits them. It's essential to identify the key benefits of the products you develop – how that product best serves the customers' wants or needs.

Unsuccessful products often have attractive features but unless those features translate into benefits, customers simply don't care. It's not a matter of "if you build it, they will come," it's a matter of meeting your customers' needs.

- **Craft your positioning and messaging**

    Product positioning should build on a product's benefits and how the product meets the needs of the target audience. You have to deeply understand what your customers value and then position your product accordingly.

    This follows through into all messaging surrounding the product. The product position may be that it's the best for meeting a particular need – the messaging communicates that positioning in a clear, concise and attention-getting fashion.

- **Define your marketing mix**

    Finally, your marketing strategy should determine how you reach your target audience – what channels and activities you include in your marketing mix. This can include traditional channels like print, radio and television, as well as digital channels, social media and mobile apps.

- **Make Optimizely part of your marketing strategy**

    Optimizely's digital experience platform and cloud-based CMS solutions should be part of your company's marketing strategy. Optimizely's online solutions help you better manage your digital assets, optimize the customer experience, and enhance your company's ecommerce efforts, improving the effectiveness of your evolving marketing strategy.

Contact Optimizely today to learn how our online marketing solutions can be part of your marketing strategy.

Note: References
1: https://www.optimizely.com

Chapter 8: New Product launch

New Product launch is the necessity of business. In this we start working on new product development when our earlier product doing satisfactory in their sale. In other words when we thinks as per our expertise the sale is on peak. In earlier chapter we have learnt about power of reinvesting. In this phase the of reinvesting will boon to the business as what we are getting profit we ought to invest in new product development through our R&D department. When we starts to work on it we must understand what type of product we need to developed and we need to developed?

During brainstorming about these question, must remember the new product ought to adhere following guideline for long lasting profit. Some of them mentioned herewith

a) It continue legacy of old successful product.

b) It has all improved areas which old product informed by feedback.

c) Cost must be optimise with quality

d) New features ought to be part of development as per client demand or time requirement.

e) If it has electronic component then understand consideration of environment must be a part of development. However every development must consider environment consideration in main factor.

f) Not to invest time and money which are already available in market with new packaging. As it will be a cheating with your customer as well as with your business.

g) All initial phase of testing and feedback must be a part of new product development as we have mentioned earlier

h) You may survey your product requirement from 3rd party before commercially launch.

- Bringing a successful product to market is a team effort. While designers are responsible for usability, utility and the rest of the user experience there are many factors which contribute to the success or failure of new product development and many of these are outside of the designer's direct control.

The figure above shows the main factors which contribute to new product development success as promoted by Gonzales and Palacios in 2002:

- Knowledge Management
- Market Orientation

- New Product Development Process
- New Product Development Speed
- New Product Development Strategies
- New Product Development Teams
- Technology
- Top Management Support

- Let us take a look at each of those factors and see how much responsibility a designer can take for them and how much lays elsewhere.

Top Management Support

At first glance, this appears to be completely out of control of the design team. After all, top managers make the decision as to what to support and what not to support right?

Unfortunately, it's not that simple. The support of top management is critical to a project's success. Without that support, budget or resources are not likely to be granted to the project and it may not get the priority it needs within the business as a whole. However, while the design team cannot force management to support their projects they can develop the political savvy to persuade management to support the best projects.

Learning to influence managers is a critical skill for design teams. Embarking on projects without managerial support is a recipe for failure but winning over support is a question of leadership and communication.

Market Orientation

Investopedia defines market orientation as follows: "**Market orientation** is a company philosophy focused on discovering and meeting the needs and desires of its customers through its product mix."

It seems reasonable to suggest that while a design team does not have control over company philosophy it should be in a good position to influence this. Conducting user research and where appropriate market research – two fundamentals of developing high quality user experiences; will enable the discovery of customer/user needs and how to meet them.

Technology

The technology used to create and deliver the product must be suitable for the market. While it is unlikely that the design team will have the final say in technology budgets or appropriation it is likely that they will be able to influence the development teams in their choice of technology.

It is clear that, for example, multi-million dollar hardware and software requirements will make a product inaccessible to the consumer market but may not be an insurmountable hurdle for government or corporate markets.

Technology must be chosen with the end-users in mind.

Knowledge Management

In many organizations today; knowledge is treated like gold dust and guarded by its owners as they would stolen treasure. Unfortunately, the creation of knowledge silos like these makes it impossible for knowledge to be effective.

Market research data, for example, can be incredibly useful to a design team but only if they can access that data and it's not kept securely in the marketing department under lock and key. Likewise user research data can be highly valuable to the marketing team but once again – only if they can access it.

Knowledge management structures will normally fall outside of the design team's remit. However, there is nothing preventing the design team from advocating for open knowledge management structures or indeed persuading senior management to support such structures.

New Product Development Strategies

Strategy, despite the way it is often abused in management speak is simply; "a plan of action designed to achieve a long-term or overall aim."

Responsibility for new product development strategies is likely to be shared between design, product management and development. This means that the design team will have some input into the strategies chosen and will be able to influence these strategies with their user research to guide the strategy to fit the needs of their users. It is probably fair to say that product management will normally have the final say on a strategic direction but designers have plenty of room to negotiate with product managers to ensure better outcomes.

New Product Development Speed

Speed to market is a critical factor in success. If your new product development process takes 5 years but your competitor's takes 2 years – it is likely that no matter how good your designs are; they will have been eclipsed by the time they get to market.

Refining the design process to maximize speed whilst protecting the user experience is a delicate balancing act and it is fully within the designer's remit. However, the development process speed is much less likely to be within the design team's control and their ability to influence that speed may be marginal at best.

Junior MBA Seeding

New Product Development Process

Having clear processes for design and development are essential. While these may be tailored to fit specific circumstances – a methodology for working that is clearly understood and agreed to by all members of the product development team is highly likely to produce better results than those created with no formal process.

The design team will, normally, have some input into these processes and be able to negotiate modifications to processes when they fail to produce optimal results. There is little control for the design team over the way other teams execute these processes. Failure in execution, from other teams, is one of the few areas where it is reasonable to say that failure was completely outside of the design team's control.

New Product Development Teams

New product development normally brings together teams of diverse people from all across an enterprise. It is strongly suggested that these diverse teams tend to be highly creative and more successful than teams of a more standardized nature.

The way teams work together is a critical factor in their success and designers operating as part of such a team have their part to play in this. Professionalism and leadership can be displayed by any member of a team (including those without official leadership and management roles) and while the design team cannot bear any responsibility for the actions of others within a team – they bear complete responsibility for their own actions.

As Michael Jordan, the world famous athlete and basketball superstar says; "Talent wins games, but teamwork and intelligence wins championships."

The Take Away

Not every factor of success for a new product development project is directly within the design team's remit. However, in the majority of cases the design team will have the ability to influence these factors and play a strong role in ensuring that the project is given the greatest possible chance of success.

The 8 key factors involved in new product development are Knowledge Management, Market Orientation, New Product Development Process, New Product Development Speed, New Product Development Strategies, New Product Development Teams, Technology and Top Management Support.

Note: **References**

1: https://www.interaction-design.org

Chapter 9: Power of Feedback

It is an important tool in any type of business. If you ignore this or never use it then your business may collapse any moment. It most important factor inside or outside the business house. We will study in detail and give seeding to the kid for overall business acumen development in life. During learning of this concept your child surprisingly give you major positive change in behaviour as he/she will use this concept in day to day life and they will take criticism in positive manner.

In my knowledge many business who are doing great have already understand power of it. In this we understand how we will take feedback so that we can use it for our positive development in business. In detail we will study here.

What is customer feedback?

Customer feedback is information clients provide about whether they are satisfied or dissatisfied with a product or service and about their general experience with a company. Customer opinion is a resource for improving customer experience and adjusting your actions to their needs. This information can be collected with surveys (prompted feedback). Still, you can also find opinions and reviews your clients post online (unprompted feedback) and collect them using Internet monitoring tools. Both sources are essential to get a complete picture of how your clients perceive your brand.

Top-performing companies understand the critical role that customer feedback plays in business. They consistently listen to the voice of their clients. They search for opinions their clients publish on social media and reviews they provide on websites designed for gathering feedback (e.g., TripAdvisor). They deliberately ask for feedback using distinct kinds of surveys. To stay ahead of the competition, you should never stop listening to customer feedback, whether positive or negative, prompted or unprompted.

LalitKaushik

Junior MBA Seeding

Reasons Why Customer Feedback Is Important To Your Business

1: Customer feedback helps improve products and services

When you introduce a new product, brand, or service to the market, you probably have an idea about customer needs. Market research that you conduct before introduction gives you an idea if potential customers would be willing to buy it, and they can also give you tips on how to improve it. However, only after your customers use your product or service, can you learn about all the advantages, flaws, and their actual experience. On top of that, their needs and expectations evolve with time.

Customer feedback is an insight into what is working well about your product or service and what should be done to improve the experience. You might have the best expertise in the industry in which your company operates, but your professional knowledge will never be more valuable to business performance than customer insights. Their opinions help you ensure that the end product will actually meet their expectations, solve their problems and fulfil their needs.

2. Customer feedback helps you measure customer satisfaction

Customer satisfaction and loyalty are crucial factors determining a company's financial performance. It is directly linked to many benefits, such as increased market share, lower costs, or higher revenue. Many studies confirmed the close connection between customer satisfaction and business performance. Therefore, there is no doubt that you want to ensure your clients are happy with your products and services. Naturally, the best way to determine if you meet their expectations is to get their opinions. Using rating-based questions, you can easily estimate the level of satisfaction and consequently predict your company's financial condition in the future.

One of the most accurate methodologies that have helped many companies measure, manage and improve customer satisfaction is **NPS (Net Promoter Score)**. The metric is based on a straightforward question that investigates how likely a customer would recommend a brand to a friend. Response options for the loyalty questions are based on a 0–10 point rating scale, with 0 representing extraordinarily negative and 10 representing extremely positive. This methodology is simple and universal, so every business can apply it in customer satisfaction management

3. Collecting customer feedback shows you value their opinions

By asking your clients for feedback, you communicate that their opinion is important to you. You involve them in shaping your business, so they feel more attached to your company. Listening to their voice helps you **create stronger relations** with them. This is the best way to gain valuable brand ambassadors who will spread positive word-of-mouth for you. And I am sure you are aware that their recommendations is probably the most effective and, at the same time, the cheapest way to acquire new customers and become more trustworthy in the eyes of your current and potential clients.

People always appreciate it when you ask them if they are happy (or unhappy) with your service. It shows you value their opinion and that you are here for them, not the other way around. They feel your primary business goal is to solve their problems and fulfil their needs, not to get their money. It puts a customer in the central position of your company, and this is the right way to run a business

4: Customer feedback helps you create the best customer experience

Today's marketing is heavily based on people's experiences with products, services, and brands. They do not buy Apple products just because they are good. They want to demonstrate their status and affiliation to a particular group. They do not buy Nike clothes because they are durable. They buy the courage to extend their boundaries. Therefore, if you focus on providing the best customer experience at every touchpoint, clients will stay loyal to your brand. And naturally, the most effective way to give them an amazing experience is to ask them what they like about your service and what should be improved.

5. Customer feedback helps to improve customer retention

A **satisfied customer** will stay with you. An unhappy customer will eventually find a better alternative to your business and leave. Customer feedback benefits are significant. It helps you determine if your clients are satisfied with your service and detect areas where you should improve. Thanks to asking for opinions regularly, you can always keep a finger on the pulse. Each time a dissatisfied customer expresses his disappointment, you can immediately react and find a solution to fix an issue. This is a perfect moment to win a client back and even increase his level of loyalty. In many cases, an unhappy customer who encountered a problem with your service but you got it fixed straightaway demonstrates more considerable devotion to your brand than a customer who has never been disappointed with your service.

6. Customer feedback is a reliable source of information to other consumers

In the times of social media, consumers do not trust commercials or expert advice so much. Opinions provided by other customers who have already used a product or service are the more reliable sources of information these days. When you look for accommodation in a city you visit, or you want to find a nice new restaurant to have dinner with friends, you read reviews beforehand. When you want to buy new shoes, you ask for your opinion on Facebook or go to a trustworthy blog to read a review. Many companies today incorporate review systems in their services and products. Think of Uber or Air Bnb. They all do their best to ensure that poor service will be detected and excluded from their business.

Customer feedback is as essential to your business as to other customers, so you should make sure that both you and your clients have easy access to opinions and reviews

7. Customer feedback gives you data that helps taking business decisions

There is no place for business decisions based on loose guesses on a highly competitive market. Successful business owners gather and manage distinct kind of data that helps them develop future strategies. Only in this way they are able to adjust their products and services to perfectly fit customer needs.

Customer feedback is one of the most reliable sources of tangible data that can further be used in taking business decisions. Customer insights will help you understand clients and their needs more profoundly. Take their suggestions into consideration, and thanks to that, find out where you should allocate your money to get the highest return on investment. You might discover that, for instance, further product development is not necessary in your case; but instead, you should focus on promoting your brand to get bigger exposure. Customer feedback is a valuable source of such data, but you must learn how to listen to it and how to translate it into actionable takeaways for your business.

If you want to stay on top of things, you should put your customers in the centre of your business and treat their feedback as the most valuable source for information in your company. They are the ones who use your products and services, so they know best what could be improved to make them even happier.

Never ignore their voice. If you fail to meet their expectations, they will find other companies which will do it better than you. Use customer feedback at all corporate levels and across all departments in your company. Insights will help you develop your products, improve customer service, and manage customer satisfaction.

(The customer's voice is priceless for your business, so never stop listening!)

In conclusion you must understand if feedback not to be biased in any condition. For this some big companies B-TO-B and B-TO-C taking help of Artificial intelligence where AI track all systems including your mobile for feedback authenticity. In this case you all are aware Amazon never except feedback of known.

Note : **References**
1: https://www.startquestion.com
2: https://www.ccl.org/articles/leading-effectively-articles/review-time-how-to-give-different-types-of-feedback/

Chapter 10: Few Entrepreneurs Successful Journey

1: Barber to billionaire taxy fleet business

Ramesh Babu the billionaire Barber born in a poor family his father was a barber who passed away in 1979 when Ramesh was just seven-year-old. His mother started walking as a made to make and meat. His father had left behind a saloon business on brigade Road Bangalore which has uncle took over he would give them five Rs. day from that. They took to having one meal a day just so they could survive. Ramesh took up various odd jobs to make a little extra cash. He would deliver newspaper and milk bottles to ease his mother's load. Sometimes in the night

Sometimes in the 90s, my mother had a big bad bitter fight with my uncle and so Ramesh started working at the salon to and learning the ropes of the business. In the morning he would be at the saloon and evening at college. Then again at night he would return to the saloon. In 1993 Ramesh babu used Maruti van. He used his journey saving to Cologne. His grandfather had to mortgage his property to enable the loan. The interest was Rs.6800 and was reeling from having to make the payment. The lady whose house his mother used to work in advised him to rent out the car instead of it just lying around

From 1994 onwards he seriously got into the car rental business. Gradually, he started adding more cast to the fleet. Till 2004 he only had about 5 to 6 cars the business was not doing well as the completion of at this level was intense. Everyone had small cars he thought of getting into luxury cars because that is sometimes something that no one else was doing.

Ramesh bought his first luxury car, in 2004, everyone told him that he was making a big mistake. 40,00,000 into 1 440 car was a very big deal. The rakes per of remarkably. No other car rental service had luxury car of his teacher. Now he has Rolls-Royce. For Mercedes. Four BMWs and 50 Toyota Innova's which he runs out. He now on his dignity fleet of 1/3

LalitKaushik

Junior MBA Seeding

five cores and his company has more than Rs.10 CR business turnover

2: Anil Aggarwal Chairman Vedanta Group

Anil Agarwal chairman and founder of Vedanta resources, has worked his way up from scrap metal dealer to billionaire.

Anil was born and brought up in Patna. He quite school at 1515 to join his father's business, making aluminium conductors. At 19 he left Patna for Mumbai to explore carrier opportunities. In the mid-1970s he began trading in scrap metal collecting it from cable companies in other states and selling it in Mumbai. In 1976 Anil acquired Shamsher Sterling Corp, a manufacture of enamelled copper among other products with a bank loan. For the next 10 years he ran both businesses.

1986, he set up a factory to manufacture jelly filled cables, creating Sterlite industries. He soon realise that the profitability of his business was volatile, fluctuating with the prices of his raw material copper and aluminium. So he decided to control his input cost by manufacturing the metals instead of buying them.

In this heat first opportunity came when the government announced a disinvestment programme. In 2001 he acquired 51% in Bartell Munim company Balco Public sector undertaking in the very next year he acquired a majority stake nearly 65% in state-run HAL both the companies her were considered sleepy and in efficient mining forms. To access international capital market Anil Agarwal and his team Inc Vedanta resources pick in 2003. At the time of its listing Vedanta resources plc was the first Indian firm to be listed on London stock exchange in 2003 Vedanta resources has a span of over four continents with its head office in London the other of Vedanta resources has a span of over four continent with his head office in London the other officer in Australia champion

Junior MBA Seeding

India Vedanta resources acquired controlling stakes in care in India. India's largest private sector oil producing from the merger of Sesa Goa's delight industries was announced in 2012 as a part of the Vedanta group consolidation.

3: From the garage to the Googleplex

The Google story begins in 1995 at Stanford University. Larry Page was considering Stanford for grad school and Sergey Brin, a student there, was assigned to show him around.

By some accounts, they disagreed about nearly everything during that first meeting, but by the following year they struck a partnership. Working from their dorm rooms, they built a search engine that used links to determine the importance of individual pages on the World Wide Web. They called this search engine Backrub.

Soon after, Backrub was renamed Google (phew). The name was a play on the mathematical expression for the number 1 followed by 100 zeros and aptly reflected Larry and Sergey's mission 'to organise the world's information and make it universally accessible and useful.'

Over the next few years, Google caught the attention of not only the academic community, but Silicon Valley investors as well. In August 1998, Sun co-founder Andy Bechtolsheim wrote Larry and Sergey a check for $100,000, and Google Inc. was officially born. With this investment, the newly incorporated team made the upgrade from the dorms to their first office: a garage in suburban Menlo Park, California, owned by Susan Wojcicki (employee no.16 and now CEO of YouTube). Clunky desktop computers, a ping pong table and bright blue carpet set the scene for those early days and late nights. (The tradition of keeping things colourful continues to this day.)

Even in the beginning, things were unconventional: from Google's initial server (made of Lego) to the first 'Doodle' in 1998: a stick figure in the logo announcing to site visitors that the entire staff was playing hooky at the Burning Man Festival. 'Don't be evil' captured the spirit of our intentionally unconventional methods. In the years that followed, the company expanded rapidly – hiring engineers, building a sales team and introducing the first company dog, Yoshka. Google outgrew the garage and eventually moved to its current headquarters (aka 'The Googleplex') in Mountain View, California. The spirit of doing things differently made the move. So did Yoshka.

The relentless search for better answers continues to be at the core of everything we do. Today, Google makes hundreds of products used by billions of people across the globe, from YouTube and Android to Gmail and, of course, Google Search. Although we've ditched the Lego servers and added just a few more company dogs, our passion for building technology for everyone has stayed with us – from the dorm room to the garage and to this very day

Note : Reference

1: www.google.com

4: Ritesh Aggarwal (CEO) OYO Rooms

Dropout who become the youngest millionaire

Born to a business class family in a be some butter, Ritesh Agrawal is an Indian and the founder CEO of Oyo Rooms and emerging branded budget Hotel network in India at the age of 13 he gave an early start to his career and travel across India while staying as a paying guest at various hotel and ends. At 17 Agarwal wrote his first book Indian engineering colleges complete in cyclopedia of top hundred engineering colleges English fourth edition Agarwal a college dropout in the first Asian to graduate as a tayi fellow 2013 the file fellowship back by the people founder Peter Hill queries it's fellows to drop out of

When India did not meet you in the very basic needs of a budget travellers taking a plunge into his opportunity Agarwal started his first venture in 2012 and found it or even stage an aggregator of bad breakfast days across India in 2013 Aggarwal transferred or able to OYO rooms where in the company standardise budget hotels in the technology enabled network to deliver hassle free Pleasant stay in the budget in economy hotels sector Oyo Rooms received hundred million US million dollars in funding from Softbank in currently offer 14,000 rooms in 18 series he his closest branded hotel compare is India's iconic Taj hotel he was named one of the top 50 and tap new in 2013 by Tata first Dot powered by New awards Ship award India Agarwal was need one of the eight hotels tennis start up full of founders in the world in 2013 by business insider Agrawal was awarded the times that nursing excellence award in 2014 OYO hotels plus to provide standardisation on 30 measures in each room including free Wi-Fi breakfast flat screen TV spotless white bad lean in office at inside count branded toiletries 6 inches showers has beverages tree and son the standards or audited every few days so that every customer is assured equality experience. OYO budget stay range from nine hundred ninety nine rupees to fifteen hundred rupees while its mid-

Junior MBA Seeding

scale room surprise so one thousand six hundred to four thousand rupees

5: Bhavish Aggarwal and Ankit Bhati

One motivational real story of an Indian startup is the story of Ola, a ride-hailing company that was founded in 2010

At the time, India did not have a strong ride-hailing industry, and the existing options were unreliable and expensive. Aggarwal and Bhati saw an opportunity to create a better solution and set out to build a ride-hailing platform that was affordable, reliable, and safe.

The journey was not easy, and the company faced many challenges, including regulatory hurdles, competition, and funding issues. However, the founders were determined to succeed and focused on building a strong team and creating a service that met the needs of Indian customers.

Their persistence paid off, and the company grew rapidly, expanding to multiple cities and offering a range of services, including bike taxis, auto-rickshaws, and food delivery. In 2019, Ola was valued at over $10 billion and had become one of the largest ride-hailing companies in the world.

The success of Ola is a testament to the power of determination, innovation, and perseverance in the face of adversity. The company's founders overcame numerous obstacles to build a service that has transformed the way people travel in India and created a company that has become a global leader in the ride-hailing industry.

Junior MBA Seeding

Worldwide Few Fellowships for students

Junior Achievement Fellowships offer an average of five (5) $10,000 fellowships each year.

- Awards are given to students with at least two years' experience in Junior Achievement, either as a mentor in high school or as an advisor in or after college. Junior Achievement is a non-profit organization dedicated to educating students in grades K-12 about entrepreneurship, work readiness and financial literacy through experiential, hands-on programs.

- Financial need is not a prerequisite for this fellowship, although the selection committee may consider it as one of several factors. The committee is primarily interested in the quality of your Junior Achievement experiences, your contributions to the program, and how the program has affected your personal and professional development.

- Fellowships are awarded annually, and current recipients must re-apply for the fellowship each academic year.

https://www.hbs.edu/mba/financial-aid/tuition-assistance/additional-harvard-funding/Pages/junior-achievement-fellowship.aspx

$1,000 Elevate Black Entrepreneurs Scholarship

- Open to Black undergraduate or graduate school student entrepreneurs who are currently building or aspire to build a new business.

https://som.yale.edu/programs/mba/affording-your-mba/funding-resources

How to Sterilize Pots for Safer Seed Raising

Raising seedlings is a great way to increase the flexibility of your garden. However, there's one major drawback. In the relatively closed system of a container, it's easy for bacteria, viruses, fungal spores, and even pest eggs to build up and pass problems from one plant to the next as the pots are reused.

Giving the pot a wash before each use and always replacing the compost is a good start towards keeping these problems in check. But for the fullest possible protection, sterilising a pot before use is a good habit to get into. Luckily, sterilising containers is very easy, either using bleach for the quickest and best results, or without bleach if you'd rather keep chemical use to a minimum. Here's what to do.

How to Sterilise Plant Pots Using Bleach

Sterilising pots using bleach is fast and effective, and is suitable for all types of pots including clay, ceramic, plastic, and even metal. Here's the basic method.

- Remove as much of the old soil as possible. To avoid waste, you can add it to your compost heap or scatter it around outdoor beds, but it's better not to re-use it for future container planting.
- Scrape off any remaining mud clumps, mineral salt deposits, mouldy patches, and so on using a blunt knife edge, a firm brush or steel wool, getting the pots as clean as possible without damaging them.
- Wash the pots thoroughly in warm soapy water, made up using an ordinary dishwashing liquid or another household soap.

Once clean, the pots can be dried off and then put into storage until you next plan to use them. Alternatively, you can continue to the sterilising stage, which is best done shortly before any repotting to keep re-infection risks down. To complete the sterilising procedure, follow these steps.

- Whenever you're using bleach or other chemicals, it's sensible to wear rubber gloves and eye protection.
- Make up a mixture of one part household bleach to nine parts water. Put the pots into the mixture and ensure they're completely covered with no air pockets, and with space for the liquid to circulate.
- Leave to soak for at least ten minutes.
- Remove the pots and rinse them thoroughly to remove all traces of the bleach solution, then place them in a bucket of fresh cold water until you're ready to use them.

After going to this trouble, it's a good idea only to use a high-quality potting compost from a reputable source, and ideally soil that's labelled as sterilised. Otherwise, you risk immediately adding new pathogens back to the freshly sanitised pots.

Sterilising without Bleach

Using bleach for sterilisation in this way is perfectly safe, but if the idea using harsh chemicals as part of your gardening seems wrong, there are a few alternative methods.

- Using Vinegar

Vinegar is less chemically harsh than bleach, and also naturally biodegrades after use to reduce the impact on the environment. What's more, you may feel more comfortable using vinegar for pots hosting edible plants, even if the risk of leaving any bleach behind is virtually zero.

The overall procedure is the same as when using bleach, but the mixture should be made up in a ratio of one part vinegar to one part water. Also, increase the soaking time to between two and three hours to take account of the relative weakness of the sterilising fluid.

- Using an Oven

Many containers can also be sterilised using heat, although this is not suitable for plastic pots, painted ceramics, or particularly delicate clay pots which could shatter on a hot surface. But for suitably sturdy containers, simply warm your domestic oven to around 100°C, place the pre-scrubbed pots on a baking tray, and slide it into the oven. Leave for an hour or so, then turn off the heat and leave the pots to cool inside the oven before removing them.

- Using Brewers' Sterilising Tablets

Lastly, if you make your own wine or beer, you'll probably already have sterilising products available such as sodium metabisulphite or another brewers' treatment. These preparations can be used perfectly well for pots so long as you follow the instructions, but they can work out expensive unless you already have a bulk supply available. However, if you have some sterilising mixture left over from a brewing session, giving your pots a quick dip is a thrifty idea.

But whether you use bleach, vinegar, heat, or the home brewer's method, making sure all the pots you use are completely free of pathogens and pests will give your container gardening a strong foundation to build on.

Tomato

Product Details

Tomato is a flowering plant cultivated for its edible fruits, which is labelled as a vegetable. There are numerous ways to grow tomatoes. They can be grown easily, cheap and healthy.

Larger varieties love to grow in open ground areas. In contrast, smaller varieties can be grown in grow bags (which have great airflow, easy to carry and are cheaper compared to other containers) pots or even in hanging baskets. But it should not be

Common Name	Tomato
Sunlight	Warmer temperature required
Water	Sprinkle water in the morning and evening
Temperature	16-30°C
Soil	Moist soil but not saturated
Fertilizer	Required
Germination	10-14 days
Harvest Season	Summer season
No. of seeds	10+

planted very close to avoid fungal attack.

Benefits / Uses of Tomato

Tomatoes are rich in vitamin B and C essential amino acids, sugar, dietary fibres, iron, potassium, vitamin K, minerals, nutrients, and good sources of phytochemical lycopene. They have the goodness of containing the anti-cancer compound lycopene. These seeds are even open-pollinated, which means the seeds can be reused from harvested tomatoes.

Specifications of Tomato seeds

Tomato seeds are small, flat, and oval-shaped, measuring about 2-4mm in length and 1-2mm in width. The color of the seeds can vary from yellow to brown or black, depending on the tomato variety.

Tomato seeds are encased in a gel-like substance that helps protect them from disease and pests. This gel can be removed through a process called fermentation, which involves allowing the seeds to sit in water for a few days until the gel dissolves.

Tomato seeds are typically viable for about 3-5 years when stored in a cool, dry place. However, the germination rate of the seeds may decrease over time, so it's best to use them within the first year or two for optimal results.

When planted, tomato seeds require warm temperatures (around 70-80°F) and moist soil to germinate. They typically take 7-14 days to germinate, depending on the temperature and soil conditions.

Planting and care for Tomato

Every tomato seed contains a tiny tomato plant that is alive but dormant, which means it's just waiting to grow. When the environmental conditions, soil and climatic conditions are right, the seed will start to germinate, and the tiny tomato plant will sprout from the tomato seed and begins to grow.

Sowing Tomato seeds

- Sow the seeds in moist soil inside a growbag, but the soil should not be over damp or soil dripping with water.
- The seed should be planted 1/4 inch deep.
- Pre-soaking of seeds in warm water overnight before planting them helps to soften the seed coat and speed up the seed germination.

Growing Tomato

- Tomato is a warm-season crop.
- It requires a warm climate and adequate moisture.
- Keep the soil moist always by slightly sprinkling the water over that area in the morning and evening.
- Overwatering in tomato plans shows early signs include cracked fruit and bumps on the lower leaves. Use grow bags with drainage holes to avoid overwatering.
- If the overwatering continues, the spots or blisters on the plant leaves turn corky.
- The soil should have good water holding capacity, aeration and It should be free from salts.
- Don't expose the germination trays or grow bags in direct sunlight until the seeds get germinated. Maintaining a warm temperature leads to faster germination than very cold or scorching weather.
- Move the grow bags to the sunlight as soon as the tomato seedlings break the surface and come out. Generally, the tomato plants will grow with branches spreading to 60-180cm (24 to 28 inches), but some are small, compact, and upright.

- Usage of organic growth promoters like panchagavya and fish amino acid help in improved flowering and overall health of the plant.

Harvesting Tomato

- 50 to 60 days are required for early-season tomatoes, 60 to 80 days are needed for mid-season tomatoes, 80 or more days are needed for late-season tomatoes.

Precautions While Growing Tomato

- Soil should be loam, sticky to give a higher yield because they have high water holding capacity.
- Soil with a pH level of 5.5 to 7.0 is most suitable for tomato production.

Common problems affecting Tomato Plants and solutions

The tomato plant will be susceptible to many pests and diseases such as early blight, fusarium wilt, late blight, bacterial wilt, verticillium wilt, mosaic virus, and Tomato hornworms.

The tobacco mosaic virus causes a common tomato disease. Handling cigarettes and other infused tobacco products can transmit the virus to other tomato plants. Leaves with a purple coloration may indicate a phosphorus deficiency, and yellow colour leaves may indicate nitrogen deficiency.

Many of the problems can be controlled by using various pesticides and fungicides and also by crop rotation. Baking soda and compost tea have fungicidal properties that can stop, resist or reduce the spread of early and late blight.

Although there are no such diseases, fertilize them with complete soluble organic fertilizer if tomato leaves become yellow and purple. The pesticides, fungicides and even various fertilizers can be purchased from online stores such as. The production rate and quality of fruit are based on the nutrients the plants get. So, the plant should be fertilized correctly and in the required quantity.

Closer spacing of plants produces higher yields than wide spacing, but too-close spacing will make air circulation diseases. Closer plantation of Tomato reduces air circulation, lower light penetration thus reduces the production rate and results in conditions.

Good drainage, sufficient light (can be given artificially), and aeration is essential for tomato seeds. If a fluorescent light is used for lighting, keep the seedlings 2 to 4 inches below the lamps; otherwise, the seeds will become saggy. Soggy soil may cause tomato seeds to rot. Insufficient light can lead to weak and spindle plants. Controlling humidity, cleaning up old plant debris, removing weeds, controlling insects, and overhead watering can help prevent all these diseases.

www.ingramcontent.com/pod-product-compliance
Lightning Source LLC
Chambersburg PA
CBHW030449220526
45464CB00006B/2455